NATIVE AMERICAN LEADERS FROM THEN UNTIL TODAY

US HISTORY KIDS BOOK

Children's American History

There were many heroes and leaders of the Native American tribes. Find out about a few of them in this book!

THE LAND OF THE FIRST PEOPLE

The first people came to North America tens of thousands of years ago. They probably walked from Asia to what is now Alaska, across a land bridge in the Bering Straits that doesn't exist any more.

NATIVES OF ELSON'S BAY

TRAVELING TO AMERICA

The people moved down through all of North, Central, and South America, establishing flourishing civilizations. By the time the Europeans "discovered the New World", millions of Native Americans were living in North America.

For a while things were peaceful between the tribes and the new settlers. But there were disagreements, and each side found it difficult to understand the other. For instance, Native Americans considered the land almost like a

living thing and tried to live in harmony with it. The Europeans thought of land as property that could be bought and sold, and from which you could grow or dig things that you could sell to make money.

NATIVE AMERICANS MIGRATING

When the Native Americans tried to resist the expansion of the Europeans' settlements, things did not go well. Read the Baby Professor book King Philip's War to learn about the first great conflict between natives and newcomers in North America.

There were hundreds of Native American tribes and cultures, all with interesting leaders and heroes. You could spend a long time learning even a little bit about the complex world in North America before the Europeans came. This book introduces you to some great Native American leaders, many of them brave people who were forced to fight to try to protect their land and preserve their way of life.

THE FIERCE WAR CHIEFS OF THE SIOUX
A GLIMPSE AT THE INDIAN CONGRESS

THE FIRST DISCOVERY OF THE WESTERN
HEMISPHERE BY THE NORTHMEN

SQUANTO

Squanto (1581-1622) was a Patuxet living in what is now Massachusetts. He got to know some Englishmen who were fishing off the coast. They kidnapped him in 1614 and took him to England to show him off. He did not get back to his land until 1619.

I n England, Squanto learned English and many other things, including how to plant a good garden by burying fish in the ground to act as fertilizer. He learned this trick from Dutch farmers, and then was able to teach it to the Pilgrims once they arrived to found the Plymouth Colony.

If people like Squanto had not helped the Pilgrims, who did not have all the skills they needed to create a new society in the new world, none of the Europeans would have survived their first winter in North America.

POCAHONTAS

Pocahontas (1595-1617) was much more than a character in a cartoon movie! She was a Powhatan woman, the daughter of the chief of her tribe in Virginia. The tribal area was near the English colony of Jamestown, and Pocahontas as a child played with children of the settlers.

POCAHONTAS (1595-1617)

POCAHONTAS SAVES SMITH

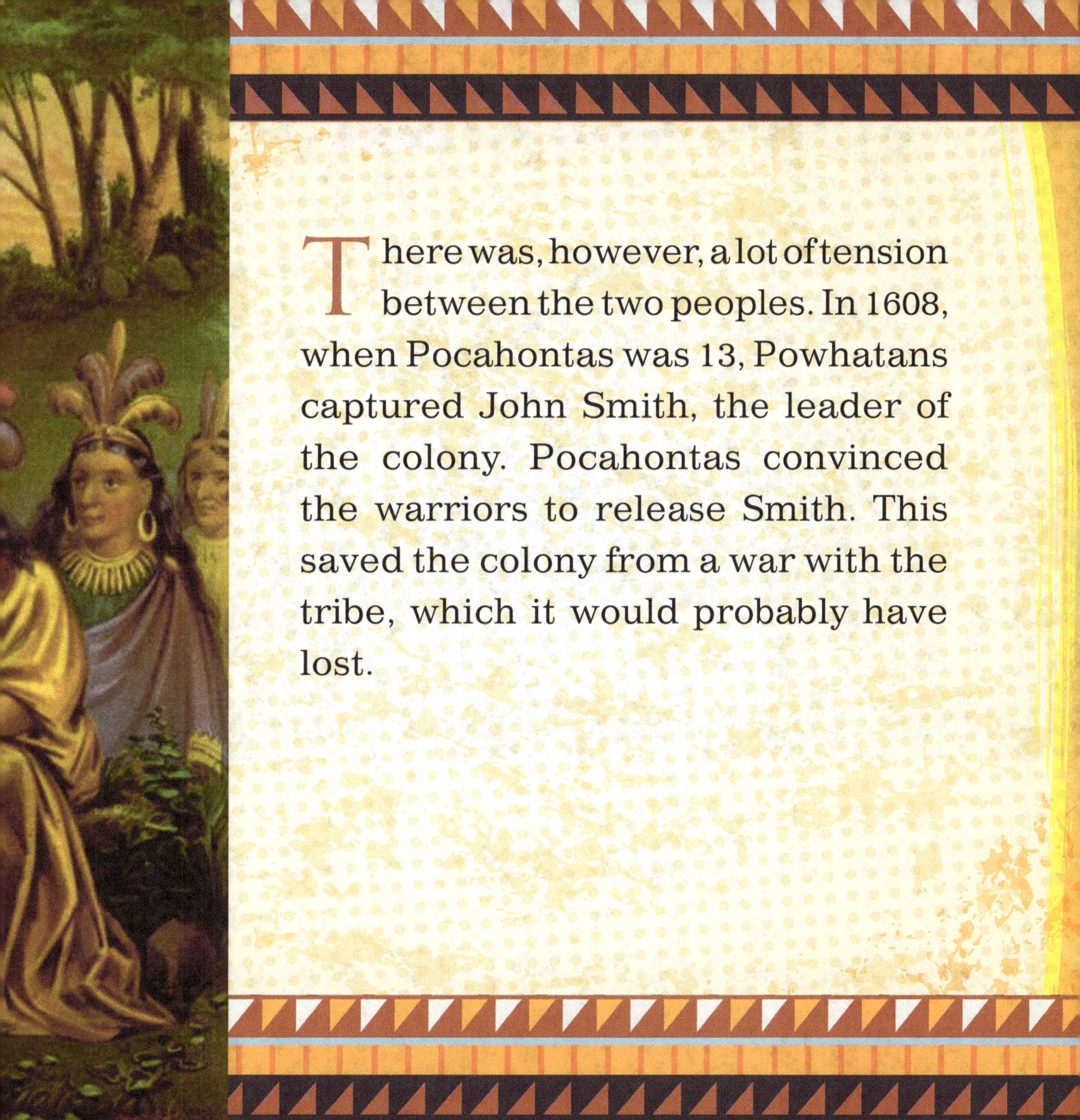

There was, however, a lot of tension between the two peoples. In 1608, when Pocahontas was 13, Powhatans captured John Smith, the leader of the colony. Pocahontas convinced the warriors to release Smith. This saved the colony from a war with the tribe, which it would probably have lost.

In 1613, Pocahontas married an Englishman, John Rolfe. This helped to make more peaceful relations between the Powhatans and the people of Jamestown. Sadly, she died of a disease just a few years later.

RECREATION OF POCAHONTAS HUGGING HER FATHER

KING PHILIP

METACOM

Metacom (1638-76) was a Wampanoag who united the tribes of New England to fight against the white settlers and to try to drive them out of tribal land. The English nicknamed him "King Philip" after the father of Alexander the Great. Read about his struggle in the Baby Professor book King Philip's War.

PONTIAC

Pontiac (1720-69) was a chief of the Ottawa tribe. He resisted the takeover of the Great Lakes area by the British army. In 1763 he led a surprise attack against Fort Detroit, capturing the fort after bloody battles. Eventually he was expelled from his tribe and was killed in what is now Illinois by member of the Peoria tribe.

PONTIAC

SEQUOIAH

SEQUOIAH

Sequoiah (1767-1843) was also known as George Guess, or Guest. He was a Cherokee silversmith in Tennessee. He invented a writing system for the Cherokee language, which up to that time had been an oral language only. This helped to preserve Cherokee culture and the tribe's sense of identity.

SACAJAWEA

Sacajawea (1788-1812) was a Shoshone woman who helped guide and interpret for the Lewis and Clark Expedition, which traveled across the west of North America in 1806.

SACAJAWEA

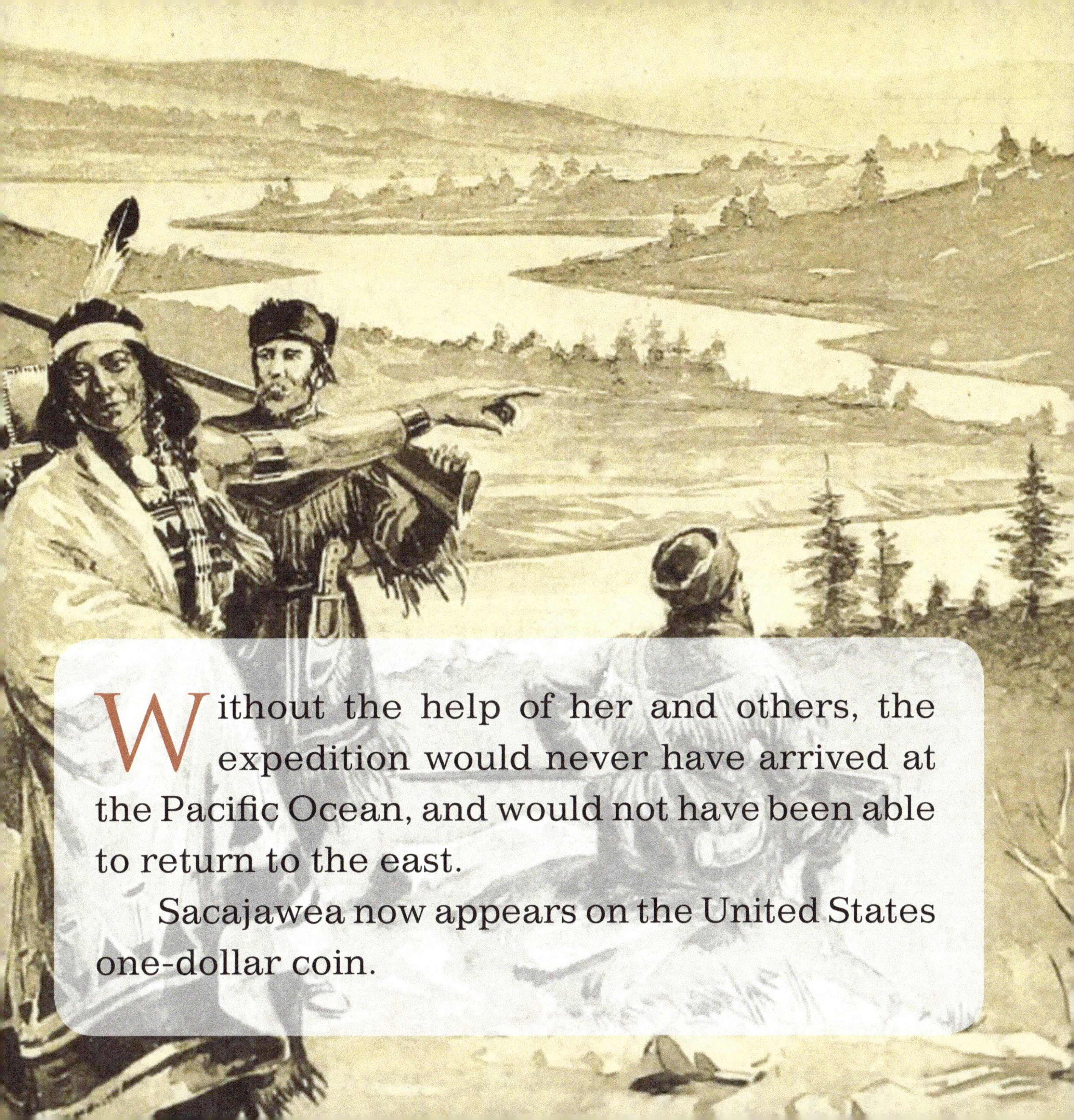

W ithout the help of her and others, the expedition would never have arrived at the Pacific Ocean, and would not have been able to return to the east.

Sacajawea now appears on the United States one-dollar coin.

TECUMSEH

Tecumseh (1768-1813) was a leader of the Shawnee people in what is now Ohio. He drew many tribes together to resist the loss of their land to Europeans. Tecumseh was part of a religious revival in 1805 in which Tenskwatawa, a shaman (holy man) called on the native people to reject taking on European ways, and to reject giving their land away.

TECUMSEH

Not all the tribe agreed with this, and Tecumseh and the followers of the revival moved north into what is now Illinois and built Prophetstown. He died during the War of 1812, fighting on the side of the British against the United States.

BLACK HAWK

B lack Hawk (1767-1838) was a war chief of the Sauk Nation in the north central United States. He was custodian of a medicine bundle that was very important to the tribe. In the War of 1812 Black Hawk led bands of fighters against the United States in support of the British. In the 1830s, "Black Hawk's War" was a series of raids and battles in Illinois and what is now Wisconsin by tribes outraged about broken treaties.

BLACK HAWK

ne result of Black Hawk's War was a push toward a policy of removing Native American tribes to land further west, and away from conflict with expanding American settlements. Read about this policy, and the terrible events resulting from it, in the Baby Professor book The Heart-Shattering Facts about the Trail of Tears.

FORT USED AS A CONCENTRATION CAMP FOR CHEROKEE BEFORE THE TRAIL OF TEARS

RED CLOUD

Red Cloud (1822-1909) was one of the best fighting leaders of the Lakota Sioux. From 1866 to 1868 he led the Lakota, Northern Cheyenne, and Northern Arapaho tribes in a series of battles against the United States Army across what is now Wyoming and Montana. What became known as "Red Cloud's War" ended in a treaty that preserved the area as Native American territory.

RED CLOUD

SITTING BULL

SITTING BULL

Sitting Bull (1831-90) was a medicine man and spiritual leader of the Lakota Sioux people. As Native Americans were resisting the advance of white settlements in the Dakotas, and the building of the first railroad across the United States, Sitting Bull had a vision. In his vision, he saw fighters from many tribes joining together to defeat the federal soldiers.

S itting Bull's vision became reality in 1875 and 1876, when northern tribes joined together to win several victories over federal armies. The capping victory was the defeat of

THE CLUSTER FIGHT

the U.S. 7th Cavalry at the Battle of the Little Bighorn. Read about that in the Baby Professor book What Happened Before, During and After the Battle of the Little Bighorn?

SITTING BULL AND BUFFALO BILL

In later years, Sitting Bull became a popular figure, appearing in Wild-West shows. Later, he was shot and killed in events that led to the last major conflict in the wars between the tribes and the federal government. Read the Baby Professor book The Wounded Knee Massacre to learn about those events.

CRAZY HORSE

Crazy Horse (1840-77) was a great fighter of the Lakota Sioux. One of his nicknames was "Curly" because his hair was not straight like that of most Native Americans. During the uprising of 1876, Crazy Horse led an attack against General Crook's forces, delaying that division long enough that it did not join up with the 7th Cavalry before the Battle of the Little Bighorn.

CRAZY HORSE

COCHISE

COCHISE

Cochise (1815-74) was an Apache leader, the chief of part of the Chricahua Apache people in what is now Arizona. From 1861 to 1872 he was one of the leaders as the Native Americans fought against United States and Mexican takeovers of their traditional lands. The "Apache Wars" ended in a treaty that preserved at least some of the lands.

GERONIMO

Geronimo (1829-1909) was another leader of the Chiricahua Apache. He was a spiritual and fighting leader, not a traditional chief. He fought against incursions into traditional Native American territory from 1850 to 1886.

GERONIMO

Often he was leading bands of no more than thirty fighters, not large armies, but his skill as a military leader let him out-maneuver U.S. armies many times larger. He led the final large

uprising of Native Americans against the federal
government, before resigning to reservation life.
Learn more about that life in the Baby Professor
book Are Indian Reservations Part of the US?

THE NATIVE AMERICAN EXPERIENCE

There is much more to learn about the people who lived in North America before the Europeans arrived. Find out more in Baby Professor books like The World is Full of Spirits – Native American Religion, Myths and Spirituality and Getting to Know the Great Native American Tribes.

Visit
BABY PROFESSOR
EDUCATION KIDS
www.BabyProfessorBooks.com
to download Free Baby Professor eBooks
and view our catalog of new and exciting
Children's Books

* 9 7 9 8 8 6 9 4 3 1 4 6 2 *